Copyrighted m

ULTIMATE **BALI**

TRAVEL GUIDE 2023

"Unlock the Secrets of the Island of the Gods: Your Ultimate Guide to Exploring Bali in 2023"

BY

ELIZABETH WALTER

Copyrighted materials

Table of Contents

WELCOME TO BALI

The sun shined brightly on the crystal blue water of the Indian Ocean as I stepped off the plane in Bali. I had heard the tales of this paradise island and was eager to experience it for myself. My first stop was the tropical forest of Ubud, which is known for its stunning beauty and incredible wildlife. As I walked through the dense foliage, I was amazed by the variety of birds and insects that surrounded me. I even spotted a few monkeys swinging through the trees!

The next day, I decided to explore the beaches of the island. I was captivated by the soft white sand and the clear waters that surrounded me. I swam in the warm ocean and basked in the sun, feeling relaxed and content.

The first thing that struck me was the stunning natural beauty of the area. Everywhere I looked, lush green forests, crystal clear blue waters, and incredible views of the ocean greeted me. It was truly breathtaking. The beaches were like nothing I had ever seen before. One of my favorite activities in Bali was snorkeling.

I was astounded by the amazing sea life I saw, like vibrant coral reefs and colorful fish. I even spotted a few sea turtles swimming in the shallows! The views of the coastline were also breathtaking. As the days passed, I explored the rest of the island. I visited the local markets and experienced the vibrant culture of Bali. I also enjoyed the delicious cuisine, from the fresh seafood to the traditional Balinese dishes.

The food was another highlight of my trip. I had the chance to try some of the most delicious Indonesian dishes, from mouth-watering street food to high-end restaurants. Irrespective of where I went, I was always treated to the freshest ingredients and most delicious flavors.

Finally, The culture of the island was another thing that made my trip so special. The hospitality of the people of Bali was simply incredible. Wherever I went, I was greeted wholeheartedly and treated like a family. The people were so friendly and welcoming, and it was a pleasure to be around them. I visited temples, markets, and other historic sites that provided a unique insight into the Balinese culture. I even took a cooking class and learned how to make some of the traditional dishes.

My trip to Bali was truly an unforgettable experience, and I would highly recommend Bali as a great place for tourists. The combination of stunning natural beauty, rich culture, and warm hospitality makes it one of the most incredible places I have ever visited.

CHAPTER I

Introduction to Bali

Welcome to the beautiful island of Bali! For centuries, this Indonesian paradise has captivated travelers with its lush jungles, pristine beaches, and vibrant culture. From the moment you step foot on the island, you'll be mesmerized by its beauty and charm. The island of Bali is an exotic blend of Hindu and Buddhist beliefs, as well as an eclectic mix of traditional and modern culture. Bali is known for its stunning landscape, with its terraced rice fields, volcanic mountains, and magnificent temples. It also offers an array of activities, including surfing, snorkeling, diving, and even trekking.

However, in addition to the magnificence of the island draws individuals here. Bali is also home to some of the most hospitable people in the world. Locals here are warm and welcoming, and the Balinese culture is all about hospitality. Regardless of where you go, you'll be met with friendly smiles and open arms. But there's more to Bali than just its beauty and hospitality.

The island also has a vibrant nightlife and a variety of delicious foods. From traditional Balinese dishes to international cuisine, Bali offers something for everyone. Bali is a magical place, and it's easy to see why so many people come here year after year. Whether you're looking to relax on the beach, explore the lush jungles, or experience the vibrant culture, Bali has something quite.

So come and explore the wonders of Bali and discover why it's one of the most beautiful and exciting destinations in the world.

A. HISTORY OF BALI

The history of Bali dates back to the Stone Age. Bali is an Indonesian island found east of Java and west of Lombok. The island is home to the Balinese people, who are known for their unique culture and vibrant way of life. This culture dates back to ancient times and has been heavily influenced by Hinduism, Buddhism and Javanese culture. Bali has been inhabited since at least 2000 BCE.

It is believed that the first inhabitants of the island were Austronesian peoples who traveled from Taiwan around this time. These people brought with them Hinduism and Buddhism that would shape the culture of the island.

The Balinese people have traditionally been farmers and fishermen, but over time they have also developed a strong artistic and spiritual culture, as well as a thriving tourism industry. In the 13th century, Bali was conquered by the Javanese Majapahit Empire and was ruled by them until the 16th century. During this period, Hinduism became the predominant religion on the island, and a unique form of Balinese Hinduism developed, blending aspects of Hinduism and Buddhism.

The Dutch East India Company arrived in Bali in the 17th century and attempted to colonize the island, but they were unsuccessful and the Balinese people managed to maintain their independence. The Dutch eventually established a trading post on the island in 1848 and signed a treaty with the Balinese ruler to gain control of the island. During the 20th century, Bali experienced a period of political turmoil, with the military dictatorship of Suharto leading to unrest and violence. This was followed by a period of relative peace and stability, and Bali has become one of the most popular tourist destinations in all of Southeast Asia.

Today, Bali is a vibrant and diverse culture, with a unique blend of traditional beliefs, modern influences and a deep appreciation for the arts and spirituality. The island is home to some of the most beautiful beaches, lush rainforests and vibrant culture in the world. Bali is an incredibly popular destination for tourists from all over the world, and it is a place where visitors can experience the magic of this unique culture.

B. GEOGRAPHY OF BALI

Bali is an island in the Indonesian archipelago located in the westernmost end of the Lesser Sunda Islands. It is located between Java to the west and Lombok to the east. Bali is bordered by the Indian Ocean to the south, the Bali Sea to the north, and the Lombok Strait to the east. The island has an area of 5,780 square kilometers and is dominated by two mountain ranges: the Barat Daya Mountains and the Barat Laut Mountains. Mount Agung, located in the east, is the highest peak at 3,031 meters and is an active volcano. The central mountain range is home to several volcanoes, and the most famous of these is Mount Batur. The coastline of Bali is indented with numerous bays, coves, and beaches that are popular with tourists.

The most famous of these is Kuta beach, located near Denpasar. Other popular beaches include Sanur, Nusa Dua, and Jimbaran. Bali has a heat and humidity with two particular seasons. The dry season runs from April to October and the stormy season from November to March. The highest temperature is usually around 30-32°C and the lowest around 20-22°C. Bali is home to a variety of flora and fauna, with a diverse range of species found throughout the island. The island is a popular destination for birdwatchers, and species such as the white-bellied sea eagle, the Javan hawk-eagle, and the wild pigeon can be found here. The island is also home to a variety of reptiles, amphibians, and mammals, such as the Komodo dragon and the Bali starling.

C. CULTURE AND PEOPLE OF BALI

Bali is an Indonesian island known for its tropical climate, beautiful beaches, and vibrant culture. The people of Bali are known for their warm hospitality and strong beliefs in the Hindu religion. The culture of Bali is unique and diverse, influenced by its Hindu roots and centuries of foreign contact, including Chinese, Dutch, and other Indonesian people.

The Balinese people have a strong sense of community and a deep respect for their fellow citizens. This is reflected in their social and cultural customs, which emphasize respect and honor for elders and family members. Balinese people practice a form of Hinduism known as Agama Tirta, which is a combination of beliefs, philosophies, and activities that stem from the teachings of Hinduism. This includes beliefs in gods, spirits, and ancestors, as well as rituals and ceremonies that are practiced throughout the year. The Balinese are also known for their art, crafts, and music. Traditional Balinese music is typically instrumental and includes a wide variety of instruments, including flutes, drums, and gongs. Music is often played at festivals and ceremonies, as well as in everyday life. Balinese art includes the intricate carvings and sculptures commonly seen on the island. Bali is also home to a number of painters, woodcarvers, and other artisans who create a range of products, from traditional artworks to modern creations. The Balinese are also known for their culinary delights, which often feature seafood, spices, and a variety of vegetables and fruits.

Balinese cuisine is an eclectic mix of flavors and ingredients, often combining elements of Indian, Chinese, and Indonesian cooking. Traditional Balinese dishes include nasi campur, a rice dish with a variety of vegetables and meats, as well as satay, a skewered meat dish often served with a spicy peanut sauce. Bali is a popular tourist destination due to its stunning scenery, friendly people, and vibrant culture. The Balinese people are welcoming and hospitable, and their commitment to preserving their culture and traditions is evident in their everyday lives. Whether you're looking to explore the natural beauty of the island, indulge in the local cuisine, or simply take in the sights and sounds of Balinese culture, Bali is sure to be an unforgettable experience.

D. THE BEST TIME TO VISIT BALI

The best time to visit Bali depends largely on what type of activities you're looking to do. Generally, the months of April to October are the best time to visit Bali as the weather is usually dry and pleasant. During these months, the temperatures stay between 25°C and 30°C (77°F to 86°F). This is also the time when Bali is packed with tourists, making it a great time to explore the island's many attractions and soak up the vibrant atmosphere.

If you're looking for more of an off-the-beaten-track experience, then the months of November to March may be the best time to visit Bali for you. During these months, the weather is slightly cooler, but still warm and pleasant. The crowds are smaller and you'll be able to explore the island's more remote areas in peace and quiet. No matter when you decide to visit Bali, you're sure to have a wonderful time. With its stunning scenery, vibrant culture, and friendly people, Bali is sure to be an unforgettable experience!

CHAPTER II

DOCUMENT REQUIREMENTS

A. Visa Requirements for Bali

Traveling to Bali requires several documents, depending on the country you are traveling from. Generally, you need a passport that is valid for at least six months beyond the date of your arrival in the country, as well as a valid visa. If you are traveling from the United States, you will need to obtain a tourist visa prior to your departure. This can be done online or at the Indonesian Embassy in Washington D.C. Tourist visas are single-entry and valid for up to 30 days.

Those from certain countries may be eligible for a Visa on Arrival (VOA). This is a visa issued upon arrival in Bali, but you must obtain and print out a Visa Approval Letter before you travel. The VOA is valid for 30 days and is non-extendable. If you plan on staying in Bali for more than 30 days, you will need to register with the Indonesian immigration office upon your arrival. This will require you to provide copies of your passport, visa, and arrival/departure card.

You must also show proof of a return or onward ticket and sufficient funds for your stay in Bali. It is also recommended that you have travel insurance valid for the duration of your trip. Depending on your country of origin, you may also need to provide proof of a valid yellow fever vaccination.

It is important to note that the requirements may change at any time and that travelers should always check the most up-to-date information prior to their departure. It is also very pertinent to be aware of all the documents you need for your trip to Bali. Failure to have the necessary documents can result in delays or even being denied entry into the country.

B.   TRAVEL   INSURANCE REQUIREMENTS

Travel insurance is an important requirement for anyone visiting Bali. It provides protection for medical expenses, lost or stolen items, trip cancellation, and other situations that may arise during a trip. It is highly recommended that all travelers to Bali purchase travel insurance before their trip.

The types of coverage available will vary depending on the provider. Generally speaking, most travel insurance policies include coverage for medical expenses, repatriation costs, trip cancellation, lost or stolen items, personal liability, and baggage delay. Some policies may also include coverage for activities such as scuba diving, surfing, and other water sports.

When purchasing travel insurance, it is important to read the policy carefully and understand what is covered and what is not. It is recommended that travelers purchase coverage that is specific to the country they are visiting, as some policies may not provide coverage for certain activities or locations.

When traveling to Bali, travelers should also be aware of the country's visa requirements. All travelers to Bali must obtain a visa prior to their arrival. The visa must be obtained from the Indonesian embassy or consulate in the traveler's home country before the trip. It is important to note that visa requirements can change, and travelers should check with their embassy or consulate for the most up-to-date information.

In addition to travel insurance and visas, travelers should also make sure to take other safety measures such as researching the area, packing light, and being aware of the local culture. By taking these steps, travelers to Bali can ensure a safe and enjoyable trip.

C. CURRENCY EXCHANGE

If you are planning to travel to Bali, then you should be aware of the currency exchange requirements for the country. The authority money of Bali is the Indonesian Rupiah (IDR). You will need to exchange your currency to Indonesian Rupiah before traveling to Bali. Most foreign currencies are widely accepted in Bali, however, ATMs and banks in Bali only accept Indonesian Rupiah.

You will need to exchange your currency to Indonesian Rupiah before you leave for your trip. You can exchange your currency at the airport, local banks, money changers and hotels.

Make sure to compare exchange rates in different places and get the best rate. It is also a good idea to carry some Indonesian Rupiah with

you before leaving your home country. When exchanging currency, make sure to keep your exchange receipts, as you will need to present them when leaving the country.

Additionally, it is important to be aware of the exchange rate of the Indonesian Rupiah before you travel to Bali, so that you can make informed decisions about your money exchange. Finally, make sure to keep your money in a safe place and be aware of any scams or fraudulent activities related to currency exchange.

D. CUSTOM REQUIREMENT

1. A valid passport: All travelers must have a valid passport with at least six months of validity left on it at the time of entry into Bali.

2. Visa: Depending on the country of origin, travelers may need to apply for a visa prior to arriving in Bali.

3. Return or onward ticket: All travelers must have a return or onward ticket when they arrive in Bali.

4. Vaccinations: All travelers should check to see if they need to get any vaccinations prior to their trip.

5. Hotel Booking or Other Accommodation: Visitors must provide proof of a hotel booking or other accommodation upon arrival in Bali.

6. Travel insurance: All travelers must have valid travel insurance that covers them for the duration of their stay in Bali.

7. Money: All travelers must have access to sufficient funds, which can be in the form of

cash, debit/credit cards, or a combination of both.

8. A valid driver's license: All travelers must have a valid driver's license if they intend to drive in Bali.

9. Transportation Booking: If you are arriving by cruise ship, you must provide proof of a return ticket to the port of origin.

E. VACCINATION REQUIREMENTS

In order to travel to Bali in 2023, travelers must meet certain vaccination requirements. All travellers must receive a vaccination certificate that meets the requirements of the World Health Organization (WHO) for an international certificate of vaccination or prophylaxis. This certificate must include the date of administration, the vaccine type and manufacturer, and the name and signature of the

administering health care worker. Additionally, all travellers must have received a yellow fever vaccine at least 10 days prior to the date of travel and must have a valid International Certificate of Vaccination or Prophylaxis (ICVP) card. It is important to note that this requirement applies to travellers over the age of 1 year.

Furthermore, it is recommended that all travellers receive a tetanus and diphtheria (Td) vaccine, a measles and mumps vaccine, and a poliomyelitis vaccine at least 10 days prior to the date of travel. These vaccines are not required, however they are recommended in order to protect against serious illnesses that are endemic to Bali.

The government of Bali has also implemented further restrictions and requirements for travelers, including completing an online health declaration form and submitting a "traveler's pass" upon arrival in Bali. Travelers may also be required to wear a face mask, maintain social distance, and follow other health and safety protocols while in the country.

Finally, it is important to ensure that all travellers have received the appropriate course of antimalarial drugs prior to travel. It is recommended that travellers speak to a health care professional prior to travel in order to determine the best course of action. Overall, these vaccination requirements are in place in order to protect travellers from serious illnesses and diseases that are endemic to Bali.

It is important to ensure that all travellers receive the necessary vaccinations and medications in order to ensure a safe and enjoyable visit to Bali in 2023. Travelers who are unable to provide proof of full vaccination will be required to take a PCR test upon arrival in Bali. If the result of the test is negative, they will be allowed to enter the country but will be required to take another PCR test five days after arrival.

Travelers may also be required to purchase a health insurance package that covers the costs of any medical treatment that may be required due to COVID-19. In order to travel to Bali in 2023, travelers will be required to provide proof of full vaccination against COVID-19. This includes providing proof of two doses of an approved vaccine and a negative COVID-19 test result

taken within 72 hours before departure. These requirements may be subject to change, so travelers should check the official government website for the latest information prior to their travel.

CHAPTER III

ACCOMMODATIONS IN BALI

Bali is an enchanting Indonesian island that offers travelers a wealth of unforgettable experiences. From its stunning beaches to its vibrant nightlife and cultural attractions, Bali has something for everyone. But one of the most important aspects of any trip to Bali is the accommodation. With a variety of options from luxury resorts to budget guesthouses, visitors to Bali can find something to suit their needs and budget. Whether you're looking for a romantic getaway, a family holiday, or a solo adventure,

Bali's accommodations offer something for everyone. From beachfront villas to modern apartments, this tropical paradise has something for every type of traveler.

A. LUXURY RESORT

Bali is one of the most popular tourist destinations in the world, and its beautiful luxury resorts are a big part of why. From beachfront villas to five-star resorts, there are countless luxurious accommodations to choose from in Bali. Whether you're looking for the perfect beachfront getaway or a unique cultural experience, there's a luxury resort in Bali that's sure to meet your needs.

For travelers looking for a luxurious beachfront experience, there are several high-end resorts along the coast of Bali. Many of these resorts offer stunning views of the ocean and a variety of amenities, such as private pools, spa services, and gourmet restaurants.

For an even more indulgent experience, some resorts offer all-inclusive packages, which include meals, drinks, and activities. If you're looking for something more unique and cultural, there are luxury resorts located in the countryside of Bali. These resorts offer a more traditional Balinese experience, featuring thatched-roof villas and private pools surrounded by lush tropical gardens. Guests of these resorts can enjoy a variety of Balinese activities, such as yoga classes and cooking classes, as well as relaxing spa treatments or a dip in a nearby beach.

No matter what type of experience you're looking for, there's a luxury resort in Bali that can meet your needs. From beachfront villas to traditional Balinese villas, there's something for

everyone in Bali. So if you're looking for a luxurious and unforgettable vacation, look no further than the luxury resorts of Bali.

B. MID-RANGE HOTELS

Bali is one of the most popular tourist destinations in the world and it is no surprise that there is a wide range of mid-range hotels available for travelers. From luxurious resorts to cozy bungalows, there is something for everyone. Whether you are looking for a romantic getaway or an adventure-filled vacation, mid-range hotels in Bali offer the perfect mix of comfort and affordability.

The first thing to consider when choosing a mid-range hotel in Bali is the location. Many of

the hotels are located in popular tourist areas such as Kuta, Legian, Seminyak, and Ubud. These areas are known for their vibrant nightlife, stunning beaches, and cultural attractions. However, some hotels are located in more remote areas, offering a more peaceful and serene atmosphere. It is important to consider the location of the hotel in order to ensure that you can easily access the attractions you want to visit.

Mid-range hotels in Bali offer a variety of amenities to ensure that your stay is enjoyable.

Many hotels offer swimming pools, spas, restaurants, and bars. Some even offer activities such as yoga classes, water sports, and cooking classes. Hotels also provide a variety of room types, from basic rooms to luxury suites.

These differences in amenities and room types can make it difficult to choose the right hotel for your needs, but it is important to consider the features and services that are important to you.

Finally, it is important to consider the price of the hotel when making your decision. Many mid-range hotels in Bali offer competitive rates, but it is important to compare prices and amenities before booking. By doing your research, you can find a hotel that fits your budget and provides the amenities you need.

C. BUDGET ACCOMMODATION

Bali is a popular destination for travelers, and budget accommodations in Bali are plentiful. Whether you are looking for a beachside resort,

a budget hotel, or a hostel, you will find an array of options to suit your needs. When booking budget accommodations, it is important to consider the location, amenities, and price. Many budget hotels offer a basic range of amenities, such as air conditioning, WiFi, a TV, and a private bathroom. Some may also offer a restaurant, pool, and other services. Hostels offer more basic amenities, such as shared bathrooms and kitchens, but may have a more social atmosphere.

When booking a budget accommodation in Bali, it is important to consider the proximity to attractions and beaches. Many of the budget hotels and hostels are located in or near popular tourist areas, such as Seminyak, Kuta, and Ubud.

This can make it easier to explore the area and take advantage of the available activities. For travelers looking for a more unique experience, there are a variety of homestays and guesthouses available throughout Bali. These accommodations are generally less expensive than hotels, and may provide an opportunity to stay with a local family and learn more about Balinese culture.

No matter what type of budget accommodations you are looking for, you will find a variety of options in Bali. From beachside resorts to basic hostels, there is something for everyone. With careful research and planning, you can find the perfect accommodation to suit your needs and budget.

CHAPTER IV

TRANSPORTATION IN BALI

Transportation in Bali is a lifeline for locals and tourists alike. This small Indonesian island is a popular destination for its stunning natural beauty, vibrant culture, and exciting activities. With its vast terrain, ranging from sandy beaches and lush rice paddies to towering volcanoes, it's no wonder that getting around Bali can be a bit of a challenge. Thankfully, there are a variety of transportation options available to visitors, including buses, taxis, and even motorcycles. With proper planning, you can easily navigate the island and experience all that Bali has to offer. Let's elaborate them one after the other.

A. GETTING AROUND ON FOOT

Getting around Bali on foot is a great way to explore the island, as it is quite compact and easy to navigate. The island is also easy to traverse, with a variety of footpaths and roads for getting around. For those looking to explore the island's cultural heritage, walking is the perfect way to do so. Bali is renowned for its ornate temples, colorful processions and vibrant street life. Exploring the island on foot allows visitors to experience these aspects of Balinese culture up close.

The best part about getting around Bali on foot is that you can take your time and really get to know the island. You can explore off-the-beaten-path sights, discover hidden

gems, and meet locals along the way. You might even stumble upon a local market, where you can sample the local delicacies. Getting around Bali on foot is an incredibly rewarding experience. It gives you the freedom to explore the island at your own pace and truly immerse yourself into the culture. Plus, it's a great way to save money. So if you're looking for an unforgettable vacation, consider walking around Bali — you won't regret it.

If you're looking to escape the hustle and bustle of the city, there are plenty of rural footpaths that offer stunning views of terraced rice paddies, lush jungles and serene beaches. Take the time to explore these hidden gems and you'll be rewarded with some of the most beautiful and remote locations on the island.

Getting around Bali on foot is generally safe, although it is important to stay alert and aware of your surroundings. Stick to well-lit paths and roads and always carry a phone or other form of communication in case of an emergency.

Walking is an excellent way to explore Bali and its many attractions. Whether you're looking to explore the island's vibrant culture or take in its stunning natural beauty, getting around Bali on foot is the perfect way to do it.

B. TAXIS AND RIDE SHARING

Taxis and ride sharing services are a popular means of transportation in Bali, Indonesia. Taxi services are available throughout the island and are a convenient way to get around. Taxis can be hailed from the street or booked in advance. Ride sharing services have become increasingly popular in recent years and are a great option for budget travelers. They offer more cost-effective and flexible options for getting around Bali. Ride sharing services are available in both urban and rural areas, and can be booked via an app or website.

When using taxi services in Bali, it is best to agree on a fare before setting off. Most taxi drivers will use the meter, but it is always best to confirm the fare before getting in the car. It is also advisable to check the driver's credentials

and make sure they are licensed with the local authorities. Taxis in Bali are usually metered and the cost of a journey can be estimated in advance, depending on the distance and traffic conditions. There is usually a minimum fare of around 25,000 Indonesian Rupiah (IDR) which is around 1.5 USD. Some drivers may ask for a higher price, especially at peak times or for longer journeys, so it's best to agree on a price before beginning the journey.

Additionally, The cost of a taxi ride from one part of the island to another will depend on the distance traveled and the type of vehicle used. Generally, you can expect to pay about $4-20 for a short trip, and around $50-100 for a longer trip depending on the type of vehicle.

Ride sharing services such as Grab, Uber and Go-Jek are also available in Bali. These services

are often cheaper than taking a taxi and are a convenient way to get around the island. Prices vary depending on the distance traveled, the type of vehicle used, and the time of day. Generally, you can expect to pay around $5-15 for a short trip, and around $25-50 for a longer trip.

When using ride sharing services, it is important to read the terms and conditions carefully before booking a ride. It is also important to check the driver's ratings and reviews before getting in the car. Ride sharing services usually offer discounts and promotions, so it is worth taking advantage of these if available. Overall, taxis and ride sharing services are a convenient and cost-effective way to get around Bali. Both services offer flexibility and convenience for

travelers, so it is important to consider both options when planning a trip.

C. RENTAL CARS

Renting a car in Bali is a great way to explore the island and experience its stunning natural beauty. With its perfect weather and endless attractions, Bali is one of the most popular holiday destinations in the world. Whether you are looking for a rental car for a day trip or a longer stay, there are plenty of rental car options available.

The cost of renting a car in Bali will depend on the type of car you choose, the length of your rental period, and the company you rent from. Generally, renting a car in Bali will cost between $20 and $50 per day, depending on the type of

car you choose. For example, a small economy car will cost around $20 per day while a mid-size SUV or minivan will cost closer to $50 per day. If you plan to rent a car for a longer period of time, you may be able to get a discounted rate. Many rental car companies in Bali also offer packages that include unlimited kilometres and other extras, such as insurance and roadside assistance.

When renting a car in Bali, it is important to make sure that you are aware of the rental car company's policies and requirements. You will need to present your valid driver's license and a valid credit card in order to rent a car. In addition, you may be required to leave a security deposit to cover any damages or additional charges.

Overall, renting a car in Bali is a great way to explore the island and experience its stunning natural beauty. With a wide range of rental car options and prices, you should be able to find the perfect car for your trip.

CHAPTER V

MUST TRY MEALS AND DRINKS IN BALI

Bali is a tropical paradise that offers an array of delicious meals and drinks that you must try! From savory dishes to sweet treats, the flavors of Bali will tantalize your taste buds and leave you wanting more. Whether you're looking for a quick bite at a local warung or a fine-dining experience, there is something for everyone. From exotic fruits to fresh seafood and traditional Balinese dishes, the culinary scene in Bali is truly unique. Not to mention, the selection of fresh juices, cocktails, and other beverages that make for a perfect accompaniment to any meal.

So come and explore the captivating flavors of Bali, and discover why this destination is a must-try for food lovers.

A. CUISINE

Bali is known for its delicious food and drinks, which are a combination of traditional Indonesian flavors and tastes from across Southeast Asia. From street vendors to fancy restaurants, there is something for everyone. Here are some of the best food and drinks to try in Bali.

1. Nasi Goreng Kampung: This Balinese dish is a must-try for anyone visiting the island. Nasi Goreng Kampung is a home-style local fried rice dish that is served with a variety of

accompaniments. It can be found at most warungs (local restaurants) around Bali and it usually costs around IDR 20,000.

2. Bebek Betutu: Bebek Betutu is a Balinese delicacy that is prepared by marinating duck with a special blend of herbs and spices, then wrapping it in banana leaves and cooking it for several hours. This traditional dish can be found at most warungs around the island and it usually costs around IDR 50,000.

3. Sate Lilit: Sate Lilit is a Balinese delicacy that is made with minced meat that is mixed with a variety of herbs and spices, then skewered and grilled over charcoal. It can be found in most warungs around Bali and usually costs around IDR 10,000.

4. Ayam Bakar: Ayam Bakar is a traditional Balinese dish that is made by marinating chicken in a blend of herbs and spices, then grilling it over charcoal. This delicious dish can be found at most restaurants around Bali and usually costs around IDR 20,000.

5. Mie Goreng: Mie Goreng is a popular Balinese dish that is made with fried noodles and a variety of vegetables. It can be found in most warungs around the island and usually costs around IDR 10,000.

6. Babi Guling: Babi Guling is a Balinese delicacy that is made by marinating pork in a blend of herbs and spices, then roasting it over charcoal. This dish can be found in most

warungs around Bali and usually costs around IDR 50,000.

7. Sate Lilit Ikan: Sate Lilit Ikan is a traditional Balinese dish that is made with minced fish that is mixed with a variety of herbs and spices, then skewered and grilled over charcoal. This delicious dish can be found at most warungs around Bali and usually costs around IDR 15,000.

8. Nasi Campur: Nasi Campur is a Balinese dish that is made with steamed rice and a variety of accompaniments such as vegetables, meats, and fish. It can be found in most warungs around the island and usually costs around IDR 15,000.

9. Lawar: Lawar is a Balinese dish that is made with a variety of vegetables and minced meat, then mixed with spices and herbs. This traditional dish can be found in most warungs around the island and usually costs around IDR 15,000.

10. Ayam Bakso: Ayam Bakso is a Balinese dish that is made with chicken and a variety of herbs and spices, then served in a soup. It can be found in most warungs around Bali and usually costs around IDR 15,000.

These are just some of the amazing must try meals in Bali. No matter where you go, you can find something delicious and unique to try. Enjoy!

B. BARS AND CLUBS IN BALI

Bali is known for its vibrant nightlife and the best bars & clubs in Bali offer an unforgettable night out. Whether you're looking for the perfect spot to party or an intimate place to enjoy a few cocktails, there's something for everyone. From the stunning beachfront bars in Seminyak to the chic rooftop bars in Kuta, Bali has something for every taste and budget. Prices range from budget-friendly to luxurious, and most places offer happy hour specials and live music. So, come out and explore the best bars & clubs in Bali and have an amazing time!

1. Ku De Ta: Located in Seminyak, Ku de Ta is one of the most iconic bars and clubs in Bali. This multi-level bar and beach club offers

world-class entertainment, stunning views of the sunset, and delicious food. Prices for drinks and food range from 20,000-80,000 IDR ($1.41-5.63 USD).

2. Sky Garden: Located in Legian, Sky Garden is a huge complex of bars, clubs, and restaurants.

It is a great place to party and dance the night away. Drinks range from 20,000-50,000 IDR ($1.41-3.53 USD).

3. Red Ruby: Located in Seminyak, Red Ruby is a trendy club with a lively atmosphere. It hosts regular music events, and the drinks prices range from 25,000-50,000 IDR ($1.76-3.53 USD).

4. La Favela: Located in Seminyak, La Favela is a popular nightlife spot with a fun, party atmosphere. The drinks prices range from 20,000-50,000 IDR ($1.41-3.53 USD).

5. Mirror: Located in Seminyak, Mirror is a chic bar and club with a great selection of music and drinks. Prices range from 20,000-50,000 IDR ($1.41-3.53 USD).

6. Coco: Located in Seminyak, Coco is a vibrant club and a great place to dance the night away. Prices range from 25,000-80,000 IDR ($1.76-5.63 USD).

7. Potato Head Beach Club: Located in Seminyak, Potato Head Beach Club is a popular beach club with a relaxed atmosphere. Prices

range from 20,000-50,000 IDR ($1.41-3.53 USD).

8. W Hotel: Located in Seminyak, the W Hotel is a luxurious bar and club with a great selection of drinks and music. Prices range from 25,000-80,000 IDR ($1.76-5.63 USD).

9. Bounty: Located in Kuta, Bounty is a great place for a night out. It is a popular spot for locals and tourists alike, and prices range from 20,000-50,000 IDR ($1.41-3.53 USD).

10. Rock Bar: Located in Jimbaran, Rock Bar is a popular bar and club with amazing views of the sunset. Prices range from 20,000-50,000 IDR ($1.41-3.53 USD).

C. BEST COFFEE SHOPS

Bali is one of the best places to enjoy coffee. There are many great coffee shops that offer amazing coffee and snacks. Some of the best coffee shops in Bali are Revolver Espresso in Seminyak, Bali Buda in Ubud, Revolver Kuta in

Kuta, and Revolver Canggu in Canggu. These coffee shops have great coffee, delicious snacks, and reasonable prices. The prices range from around $2-$7 depending on the coffee and the location.

1. Bali Pulina Coffee Plantation: Located in the Gianyar district, Bali Pulina Coffee Plantation is a coffee estate where you can learn about the traditional Balinese coffee-making process and purchase freshly brewed coffees.

They offer a variety of coffees, including traditional Balinese coffee, Robusta, Arabica, and espresso. Prices range from 40,000 to 80,000 Indonesian Rupiahs (IDR).

2. Cafe Organic: Cafe Organic is a charming cafe located in the heart of Ubud. They specialize in organic coffees and teas, made with beans sourced from local farmers. Prices range from 30,000 to 60,000 IDR.

3. Bali Buda Cafe: Located in the Seminyak area, this cafe offers a wide range of coffees and teas, as well as a variety of snacks and desserts. Prices range from 30,000 to 70,000 IDR.

4. The Coffee Library: This cafe is located in Kuta, and is known for its cozy atmosphere and delicious coffees. Their menu includes espresso, cold brew, and more, and prices range from 40,000 to 80,000 IDR.

5. Revolver Espresso: This cafe is located in Seminyak, and they specialize in serving up high-quality espresso. Prices range from 30,000 to 70,000 IDR.

6. Bali Coffee & Tea House: Located in Canggu, this cafe offers a variety of coffees, teas, and snacks. Prices range from 40,000 to 80,000 IDR.

7. The Space Bali: This cafe is located in Seminyak, and offers a wide selection of coffees

and teas, as well as other snacks and desserts. Prices range from 30,000 to 80,000 IDR.

8. Cafe Organic Bali: This cafe is located in the Ubud area and offers organic coffees, teas, and snacks. Prices range from 30,000 to 60,000 IDR.

9. Kopi Bali House: This cafe is located in Seminyak, and offers a wide selection of coffees and teas, as well as other snacks and desserts. Prices range from 40,000 to 70,000 IDR.

10. Bali Coffee Roastery: Located in Ubud, this cafe specializes in locally-roasted Indonesian coffees and teas. Prices range from 30,000 to 70,000 IDR.

CHAPTER VI

POPULAR TOURIST ATTRACTIONS IN BALI

A. POPULAR BEACHES FOR TOURISM

Bali is known for its stunning beaches, spectacular scenery, and vibrant culture, making it a popular destination for tourists from all over the world. Its many beaches offer a variety of attractions for tourists, from sunbathing and swimming to snorkeling and surfing. Here are some of the most popular beaches and attractions for tourists in Bali.

1. Kuta Beach: Kuta Beach is one of the most popular beaches in Bali, and it attracts tourists from all over the world. It has golden sand, clear blue water, and plenty of activities for everyone, like surfing, beach volleyball, and parasailing. Kuta Beach is also a great spot for sunset and sunrise watching.

2. Sanur Beach: Sanur Beach is located on the eastern side of Bali, and it's a great beach for swimming and sunbathing. It also has great snorkeling and diving spots, and you can spot a variety of colorful fish and coral. Sanur Beach is also known for its traditional fishing boats and its vibrant nightlife.

3. Nusa Dua Beach: Nusa Dua Beach is a popular beach for tourists, and it's known for its crystal clear waters and white sand. It's a great spot for swimming, snorkeling, and paddle boarding. It's also home to a number of luxurious resorts and beach clubs.

4. Seminyak Beach: Seminyak Beach is a great spot for surfers, and it's known for its excellent waves. It's also popular for its vibrant nightlife, with lots of bars, restaurants, and nightclubs. Seminyak Beach is also a great spot for sunset watching.

5. Uluwatu Beach: Uluwatu Beach is a great spot for surfers, as it has some of the best waves in Bali. It's also a great spot for sunset watching, and it's known for its stunning scenery. The beach is also home to the iconic Uluwatu Temple, which is a popular tourist destination.

B. RELIGIOUS SITES OF ATTRACTIONS

Bali is a popular tourist destination known for its beautiful beaches and relaxed atmosphere. It is also home to a number of religious sites of attraction, making it a great destination for those who wish to explore the spiritual side of the island. These are;

1. Tanah Lot Temple: Tanah Lot is one of the most iconic temples in Bali and is located on a small rock island off the coast of the Balinese mainland. It is one of the most popular religious sites for tourists, and is a great place to visit for its beautiful views and its spiritual significance.

2. Uluwatu Temple: Uluwatu Temple is one of the six key temples in Bali, and is believed to be the spiritual center of the island. With its unique beauty and stunning views, it is a popular tourist destination.

3. Besakih Temple: Besakih Temple, situated in the tranquil village of Besakih, is the largest and holiest Hindu temple in Bali. The temple complex is highly significant and is a great place to experience Balinese Hindu culture.

4. Pura Ulun Danu Bratan: Pura Ulun Danu Bratan is one of the most picturesque temples in Bali, as it is situated on the edge of Lake Bratan in the mountains of Bali. It is a popular tourist destination and is a great place for spiritual reflection.

5. Pura Tirta Empul: Pura Tirta Empul is a temple which is renowned for its holy springs, which are believed to have medicinal powers. This temple is a great place to visit to experience the spiritual energy of Bali.

6. Pura Lempuyang: Pura Lempuyang is one of the oldest temples in Bali and is located on the slopes of Mount Lempuyang in East Bali. The temple is highly revered and is known for its incredible views of the surrounding landscapes.

7. Pura Besakih: Pura Besakih is one of the most important temples in Bali and is believed to be the spiritual center of the island. With its stunning architecture and spiritual significance, it is a great place to visit for tourists.

8. Pura Luhur Uluwatu: Pura Luhur Uluwatu is considered to be one of the most sacred temples in Bali and is located on the western tip of the island. It is a great place to experience Balinese culture and spirituality.

9. Pura Ulun Danu Batur: Pura Ulun Danu Batur is one of the most important temples in Bali and is located on the slopes of Mount Batur in Kintamani. It is a great place to visit for its incredible views and spiritual significance.

10. Pura Batu Bolong: Pura Batu Bolong is a temple located on the beach near Canggu and is a great place to experience both the spiritual and cultural aspects of Bali. It is a great place to relax, meditate and take in the beauty of the surrounding landscapes.

C. SHOPPING AND NIGHTLIFE ATTRACTIONS IN BALI

Bali is one of the world's premier tourist destinations, offering a wide range of shopping and nightlife experiences. From the traditional markets of Ubud to the chic boutiques of Seminyak, there's something for everyone. Bali is also known for its vibrant nightlife, with beachfront bars, world-class nightclubs, and live music venues. Here are some of the best shopping and nightlife attractions in Bali.

Shopping:

Ubud Market – Ubud is the cultural heart of Bali and the Ubud Market is the perfect place to find traditional Balinese souvenirs. You can find handmade clothes, jewelry, wood carvings, and more.

Seminyak Square – Seminyak Square is a modern shopping center, with designer stores, fashion boutiques, and restaurants. It's the perfect place to find luxury items at the best prices.

Kuta Art Market – The Kuta Art Market is a great place to find unique art and craft items. Here, you'll find a variety of paintings, sculptures, and local handmade products.

Nightlife:

Ku De Ta – Ku De Ta is one of the most popular beach clubs in Bali. The venue features live DJs, cocktails, and stunning views of the ocean.

Sky Garden – Sky Garden is a lively nightclub located in the heart of Kuta. It features live music, international DJs, and a variety of drinks.

Single Fin – Single Fin is a popular surf bar located in Uluwatu. The venue features live music, stunning views of the ocean, and a variety of food and drinks.

These are some of the best shopping and nightlife attractions in Bali. Whether you're looking for traditional Balinese souvenirs or an unforgettable night out, Bali has something for everyone.

CHAPTER VII

ADVENTURE ACTIVITIES IN BALI

Bali is a paradise for adventure seekers, offering an incredible array of experiences that appeal to a wide range of thrill-seekers. From adrenaline-pumping water sports to hair-raising hikes, the island has something for everyone looking for an adrenaline rush. From white-water rafting and canyoning to surfing and paragliding, Bali has it all. Whether you're looking for a high-octane adventure or a more relaxed experience, you're sure to find something that will take your breath away. With its stunning natural beauty and unique culture, Bali is the perfect place to explore and experience a thrilling adventure.

A. HIKING AND TREKKING

Hiking and trekking are two popular adventure activities in Bali. The island's lush green hills and valleys are home to some of the most spectacular scenery in Indonesia, making it the perfect destination for outdoor enthusiasts.

There are plenty of trails to explore, ranging from easy day hikes to multi-day treks. Popular routes include the Mount Batur volcano trek, the Tegallalang Rice Terraces trek, the Mount Agung trek, and the Mount Rinjani trek. Each one offers a unique experience, with stunning views, diverse wildlife, and fascinating cultural sites.

One of the most popular hikes is the Mount Batur trek. This trek takes you up the volcano and offers stunning views of the nearby lake and village. This trek is suitable for all levels of hikers and takes about four to five hours to complete.

Another great hike is the Ubud Monkey Forest Trek. This trek takes you through the Ubud Monkey Forest, where you can see hundreds of wild monkeys living in the trees. This route is suitable for all levels of hikers and takes about two to three hours to complete. Hiking and trekking in Bali also provide a great way to get to know the local communities.

Many tours include visits to Balinese villages and temples, giving hikers the opportunity to learn about the culture and customs of the island.

No matter what type of trek you choose, safety should always be your top priority. Make sure you are prepared with the right supplies and clothing, and never hike alone. You should also check the weather before setting out, and be aware of the potential risks of altitude sickness and extreme temperatures.

Hiking and trekking in Bali provide an unforgettable adventure. Whether you're looking for a challenging expedition or a leisurely stroll, you'll find plenty of amazing trails to explore. So lace up your hiking boots and get ready to explore the beautiful island of Bali!

B. CYCLING

Cycling is one of the most popular adventure activities in Bali. The island is blessed with a stunning landscape, with lush green rice fields, beautiful beaches, rugged mountains, and stunning temples. Cycling in Bali gives visitors the opportunity to explore the island in a unique way, taking in the sights, sounds, and smells of the island. Whether you're a beginner or an experienced cyclist, there are cycling routes to suit all levels. The Ubud Cycling Tour is a popular route, taking you through the beautiful Balinese countryside. This route starts at Ubud, and goes through the stunning rice fields of Tegallalang, the Kintamani Volcano, and the jungle-clad temples of Bedugul.

The Batur Cycling Tour is a bit more challenging, with a route that takes you up the slopes of Mount Batur. This route offers spectacular views of the volcanoes and lakes of Bali, and is a great way to get a unique perspective of the island's natural beauty.

For those looking for a more leisurely cycling experience, there are plenty of routes along the coastline and other parts of the island. These routes offer stunning views of the beaches, temples, and villages of Bali. Irrespective of your experience level, cycling in Bali is an unforgettable experience. With its stunning scenery, welcoming people, and unique culture, Bali is the perfect place to explore by bike.

C. WATER SPORTS

Water sports are a great way to experience the beauty and adventure of Bali. From snorkeling and scuba diving to surfing and rafting, there is something for everyone. Snorkeling is one of the most popular water sports in Bali. The island is home to a wide variety of marine life, making it an ideal spot for exploring the underwater world. There are a number of snorkeling spots around the island, ranging from shallow reefs to deep water. Snorkelers can explore coral reefs, sea turtles, and tropical fish.

Scuba diving is another great way to explore Bali's underwater world. Divers can find a variety of marine life, including manta rays, sea turtles, and even reef sharks.

Diving in Bali is suitable for all levels, ranging from beginner to advanced. Surfing is another popular water sport in Bali. The island is home to some of the best surfing spots in the world, with waves suitable for beginner, intermediate, and advanced surfers. Surfers can find a variety of surf spots, ranging from long, rolling waves to powerful, barrel-shaped waves. For a more extreme water sport, rafting is available in Bali. The island offers some of the best white water rafting in the world, with a variety of rapids suitable for all levels of experience. Bali also offers a variety of other water sports, such as kayaking, windsurfing, and stand-up paddle boarding. No matter what water sport you choose, Bali has something to offer. So, come and explore the amazing beauty and adventure of Bali with a variety of water sports.

CHAPTER VIII

TIPS FOR A SUCCESSFUL TRIP BALI

Bali is an amazing destination for travelers looking for a paradise getaway. With its breathtaking scenery, amazing culture and friendly locals, it is no wonder why so many people flock to this beautiful island. Planning a successful trip to Bali requires careful consideration of many factors. Are you ready to experience the exotic beauty of Bali?

Whether you are a first-time visitor or a returning one, there are some key tips that can help you make the most of your trip. From booking the right accommodation to choosing the right activities, which have been stated previously in this guide book. In addition, this guide book will provide you with some valuable insights on how to make your trip to Bali a truly memorable experience and a successful one.

A. HEALTH AND SAFETY

Health and safety should always be a priority when travelling. Bali is a very popular destination and as such, it has a good infrastructure, however, there are still some risks associated with travelling to the island.

Firstly, it is important to make sure that you are up to date with all of the necessary vaccinations and immunisations before you go. It is also recommended that you purchase travel insurance to cover any medical costs that may arise.

When it comes to health and safety, it is important to take precautions against mosquito bites and other insect-borne diseases. Wear light-coloured clothing and use insect repellents when outdoors. It is also important to avoid swimming in freshwater pools and to drink only bottled water.

It is likewise essential to know about the neighborhood regulations and customs. It is best to avoid public displays of affection and to dress appropriately. It is important to stay vigilant when travelling in Bali and to trust your instincts. If you think something is not right, then it is best to leave the area.

Finally, it is important to stay in touch with family and friends and to have a reliable form of communication. Make sure that emergency contacts are readily available. By following these health and safety tips, you can ensure a successful and enjoyable trip to Bali.

B. MONEY AND BUDGETING

Money and budgeting are essential tips for a successful trip to Bali. Having a clear budget will help you manage your finances and ensure you don't spend too much. Before you set off, it's important to research the cost of items in Bali, such as accommodation, food, and activities. Consider the type of trip you want to have - if it's a luxury trip, you should be prepared to spend more.

It's also important to factor in hidden costs, such as transportation and tips for services. To ensure you stick to your budget, set a daily limit and keep track of your spending. You may also consider bringing a prepaid travel card, which will allow you to easily monitor and control your spending. Additionally, make sure you have a backup plan in case of emergency - this could include taking out travel insurance or having access to additional funds. With careful planning and budgeting, you can have a successful and enjoyable trip to Bali.

C ETIQUETTE AND CUSTOMS

Etiquette and customs are an important part of any trip to Bali. It is essential to be aware of the expected behavior and cultural norms to ensure a successful and respectful trip.

First, it is essential to understand the differences between Balinese Hinduism and the religion practiced in most Western countries. Balinese Hindus practice a form of Hinduism that is unique to the island, and visitors should be aware of this and be respectful of the culture. It is critical to dress unobtrusively and to keep away from public presentations of warmth. It is also important to be aware of local holidays and celebrations, and to not disrupt them.

Second, it is important to be aware of the different customs in Bali. For example, it is customary to take off your shoes before entering a temple or home. It is also important to be aware of the local language and to use it when interacting with locals. Additionally, it is important to be aware of gift-giving customs, and to not bring gifts that could be seen as insulting or offensive.

Finally, it is essential to be aware of the etiquette when dining in Bali. It is polite to wait to be invited to sit down at the table, and to not start eating until the host has begun. It is also important to not leave food on your plate, as this is seen as disrespectful. Additionally, it is important to be aware of the local customs when it comes to drinking alcohol, as drinking in public is not allowed. Overall, understanding the etiquette and customs of Bali is essential for a successful trip. It is important to be aware of the local culture, dress modestly, use the local language, and be mindful of gift-giving and dining etiquette. By following these tips, travelers can ensure a respectful, successful, and enjoyable trip to Bali.

D. POSSIBLE SCAMS IN BALI

When traveling to Bali, it's important to be aware of possible scams that could take place during your trip. To ensure a successful trip to Bali, here are some tips to keep in mind:

1. Watch Out for Overcharging: Tour guides and drivers may try to overcharge tourists for their services. Before agreeing to any tour or ride, make sure you know the exact cost and are comfortable with it.

2. Don't Buy Souvenirs From Unofficial Shops: Official souvenir shops may charge more than unofficial shops, but they are more reliable and are less likely to be scams.

3. Don't Buy Jewelry From Unofficial Stores: Jewelry in Bali is usually very cheap, but it may not be authentic. If you see jewelry for a price that seems too good to be true, it likely is.

4. Don't Take Photos with Strangers: Some locals may try to get tourists to take photos with them and then demand money for it. Politely decline and avoid this scam.

5. Be Wary of Fake Money: Counterfeit money is a problem in Bali. Make sure to check any money you receive, and if anything looks suspicious, don't accept it.

6. Don't Buy Drugs: Drug dealing is illegal in Bali, and those caught can face serious consequences. Avoid this scam at all costs.

7. Fake Street Vendors: Street vendors in Bali are often selling counterfeit goods. Be sure to inspect any item you purchase before handing over any money.

8. Fake Tour Guides: There are many fake tour guides operating in Bali, who often charge exorbitant fees for services that are not always provided.

Always ask for credentials and research any company you plan to hire before paying any money.

9. Fake Drivers: Some drivers in Bali are unscrupulous and will attempt to overcharge tourists for rides. To avoid this, always agree on a price before getting in the vehicle.

10. Fake ATMs: There are a number of ATMs in Bali that will take your card and money, but will not provide any cash. Be sure to use only trusted ATMs.

11. Fake Hotels: There are many hotels in Bali that are not what they appear to be. Always check reviews, photos and prices before booking a room. By following these tips, you can ensure a safe and successful trip to Bali.

CHAPTER XI

ADDITIONAL 30 TRAVEL ADVICE

Are you ready to explore the stunning island of Bali? This Indonesian paradise is a must-visit destination for anyone looking for a unique and unforgettable vacation experience. From stunning beaches and lush jungles, to vibrant nightlife and ancient temples, Bali is a place unlike any other. To ensure that you make the most of your time in this magical destination, here are some essential and additional travel advices to help you get the most out of your trip.

1. Always check the latest travel advice before you go to Bali.

2. Make sure you get the right travel insurance before you go.

3. Bring a good supply of sun cream and insect repellent.

4. Be mindful of the local culture and customs and respect them.

5. Take out enough cash before you go, as ATMs can be unreliable.

6. Familiarise yourself with the local laws and regulations.

7. Choose your accommodation wisely.

8. Keep an eye on your belongings, as pickpockets are common.

9. Don't drink the tap water.

10. Learn some basic Indonesian phrases to help you get around.

11. Research the best areas to visit before you go.

12. Make sure you know the current visa requirements.

13. Choose local transport such as scooters and taxis.

14. Use official taxi companies such as Bluebird and Grab.

15. Use your hotel safe to keep your valuables secure.

16. Take out travel insurance to cover any medical expenses.

17. Don't be tempted to buy counterfeit goods.

18. Get vaccinated against common diseases before you go.

19. Don't be scared to try the local cuisine.

20. Be aware of the potential risks of scuba diving.

21. Keep yourself hydrated in the hot weather.

22. Take a good supply of mosquito repellent.

23. Wear modest clothing when visiting temples and sacred sites.

24. Be prepared to haggle when shopping in markets.

25. Avoid swimming in areas with strong currents.

26. Carry a photocopy of your passport with you at all times.

27. Don't leave your belongings unattended in public places.

28. Make sure your accommodation has air conditioning.

29. Don't attempt to drive a motorbike if you're not experienced.

30. Have fun and make some amazing memories!

CHAPTER

CONCLUSION

Bali is an amazing destination that should be on everyone's travel bucket list for 2023. With its stunning beaches, lush rainforests, terraced rice fields, vibrant culture, and endless activities, it's the perfect place to explore and have an unforgettable experience. From the iconic temples of Uluwatu and Tanah Lot, to the lush Ubud rice paddies and the intriguing Ubud Monkey Forest, the beauty of Bali is unrivaled. Whether you're looking for an adventure-filled holiday, a romantic getaway, or a tranquil retreat, Bali has something to offer.

The people of Bali are warm and welcoming, and they take great pride in sharing their culture and traditions with visitors. From the traditional dance performances and vibrant markets, to the soothing yoga and meditation classes, Bali is an ideal place to rejuvenate and find balance. With its world-class restaurants, luxurious spas, and bustling nightlife, Bali is also a great destination for those seeking to party and have a good time.

Whether you're a first-time traveler or a seasoned pro, a trip to Bali in 2023 will be an unforgettable experience. With its stunning landscapes, vibrant culture, and endless activities, this tropical paradise is the perfect place to explore and make memories for a lifetime.

Printed in Great Britain
by Amazon

26015897R00059